Small Wonders

Also by Lynne DeMichele

Treasure in Clay Jars

Small Wonders

Children's Faith Stories

From the Indiana United Methodist Church

Compiled and Edited by
Lynne Bevan DeMichele

PROVIDENCE HOUSE PUBLISHERS
Franklin, Tennessee

Printed in the United States of America

05   04   03   02   01   1   2   3   4   5

Library of Congress Catalog Card Number: 00-110727

ISBN: 1-57736-225-X

Cover design by Gary Bozeman

Cover art by Jinny Barr

PROVIDENCE HOUSE PUBLISHERS
238 Seaboard Lane • Franklin, Tennessee 37067
800-321-5692
www.providencehouse.com

For Such is the Kingdom

Whoever will not welcome the realm of God as a little child welcomes it will not enter into it. My father was once walking on the beach with his three-year-old grandson when the little boy stopped, picked up a tiny fragment of a seashell, and began to examine it. My father bent down, and looking at the tiny fragment, he asked the boy, "How could you see such a little shell?" "Because," said the boy, "I have little eyes."

—THOMAS W. MANN
To Taste and See

Contents

Foreword

My five-year-old grandson, Dimitrius, is quite a precious lad, and continues to amaze his granddad with his insights and ability to articulate his ideas. He loves going to church and is active in a number of activities, among them the children's choir.

Some months ago, he was rehearsing a song his choir was to sing the following Sunday. My twelve-year-old son, Bryan, a bit more mischievous and somewhat "irreverent," began to tease Dimitrius and to mock his singing.

Dimitrius, indignant and stern in his five-year-old way, said to Bryan with a tone befitting an older child, "Bryan, you'd better stop that, this is God's song . . . !"

This is God's song! And so it was, a song of praise to God. Little Dimitrius was singing it with all his heart, his voice ringing out in glad and happy tones. God's song, and God's child.

There are so many unbelievable news accounts of little children being neglected, abused, abandoned, even killed. Each time I read such an account, I want to shout out like little Dimitrius, indignant, and pained, "You'd better stop that, these are God's children!"

God's children. Loving, innocent, and naïve. Like my little grandson, insightful; and like my son, Bryan, playful and mischievous. But precious all! Whatever their race or age, social or economic background, ethnic group or religion, children are God's special gift to humanity.

In this book, children from United Methodist congregations across Indiana talk to us and to each other. They also talk to and about God, faith, life, and childhood. Parents and those who work with children also share stories about them.

Children make us laugh, think, and cry. As you read this volume you'll probably do all three, as did I.

As a Bishop, children with whom I interact in church and other settings across the state, as well as in my own home, have a way of "bringing me down to size!" Bishop for them is neither a barrier nor intimidating. Somehow they remind me of the child in me. Vulnerable and hopeful.

I trust that in listening to the voices of the children in this volume, you will discover again the child in you. And that you will remember above all else that you are God's child. At whatever age or stage in life, you are God's child; whatever circumstances or challenges you face, you are God's child— precious in God's sight. The children remind us.

WOODIE W. WHITE, BISHOP
Indiana Area
The United Methodist Church

Introduction

Our birth is but a sleep and a forgetting;
The Soul that rises with us, our life's Star,
Hath had elsewhere its setting,
And cometh from afar;
Not in entire forgetfulness,
And not in utter nakedness,
But trailing clouds of glory do we come
From God, who is our home;
Heaven lies about us in our infancy!

—WILLIAM WORDSWORTH
Ode on Intimations of Immortality
from Recollections of Early Childhood

Jesus clearly loved children. He saw in them the power of a simple faith, of approaching God with trust and belief "as of a child." At some point in our lives, we have each undoubtedly experienced the delight of an unexpected bit of wisdom issuing from the mouth of a youngster—"out of the mouths of babes . . ." (Ps. 8:2).

This volume represents a gathering of such anecdotes and small stories. They are drawn from parents, teachers, friends, and from the children themselves—stories which reveal a bit of that certain "glory" Wordsworth refers to in his poem. Each anecdote suggests something new and precious about life and death, and a few unalterable truths discovered in between. Many of the items come from Indiana, as that is where this collection was initiated—a project of the United Methodist Bishops' Task Force on Children & Poverty. We hope you will take your time as you read and absorb these stories of children who have acted on faith, expressed their understanding of God and the transcendent, and who—in their brief time on earth—see things with new eyes, still "trailing clouds of glory" from the presence of God who has entrusted them to our care.

You will notice in the collection some unattributed anecdotes which were sent to us via electronic mail. Each likely followed a branching trail of numerous e-mail relays from friend to friend, colleague to colleague. A happy phenomenon of today's cyber culture is that good stories can be widely circulated and shared with a quick tap of a computer key. Unfortunately, a casualty of this kind of sharing is that authorship is often lost. Regrettably, we don't know to whom these stories can be credited.

In spite of their apocryphal nature, each contains a pure, sweet truth—one worth passing along. Our sincerest thanks go out to those who submitted stories for this project and to the unknown individuals who understood their value enough to commit them to writing and send them into cyberspace.

LYNNE DEMICHELE
Editor

PART ONE

From the
Mouths of Babes

What Kids Know about Love

In a survey of four- to eight-year olds, kids shared their views on love. Here are some of their answers:

When my grandmother got arthritis, she couldn't bend over and paint her toenails anymore. So my grandfather does it for her all the time, even when his hands got arthritis too. That's love.

When someone loves you, the way she says your name is different. You know that your name is safe in her mouth.

Love is when you go out to eat and give somebody most of your french fries without making them give you any of theirs.

Love is when someone hurts you. And you get so mad but you don't yell at him because you know it would hurt his feelings.

Love is when my Mommy makes coffee for my daddy and she takes a sip before giving it to him, to make sure the taste is OK.

Love is what's in the room with you at Christmas if you stop opening presents for a minute and look around.

If you want to learn to love better, you should start with a friend who hates you.

There are two kinds of love—our love and God's love. But God makes both kinds of them.

Love comes from people's hearts, but God made hearts.

Love goes on even when you stop breathing and you pick up where you left off when you reach heaven.

You really shouldn't say "I love you" unless you mean it. But if you mean it, you should say it a lot. People forget.

I let my big sister pick on me because my Mom says she only picks on me because she loves me. I wish I could have picked on my baby brothers because I love them.

You never have to be lonely. There's always somebody to love, even if it's just a squirrel or a kitten. You can break love, but it won't die.

AUTHOR UNKNOWN

The Never-Ending Hug

My youngest daughter Laura said to me once, "I think maybe heaven will be like a loving hug that never ends."

She said this when we were having our nighttime routine of chatter, prayer, and hugs. She especially likes a long hug. She said, "That's the best part!"

The hug—that's when the love becomes more than words, doesn't it? When the action expresses God's love—that's when it touches our hearts most. We want to savor it! We don't want it to end.

Our individual bit of spirit is wrapped up in God's abundant spirit, the best place of all to be—in a never-ending hug!

DEBBIE (MAHAN) RUSSELL
Frankfort, Indiana

Explaining God

One of God's main jobs is making people. He makes them to replace the ones that die, so there will be enough people to take care of things on earth. He doesn't make grown-ups, just babies. I think because they are smaller and easier to make. That way He doesn't have to take up His valuable time teaching them to talk and walk. He can just leave that to mothers and fathers.

God's second, most important job is listening to prayers. An awful lot of this goes on, since some people, like preachers and things, pray at times beside bedtime. God doesn't have time to listen to the radio or TV because of this. Because He hears everything, there must be a terrible lot of noise in his ears, unless he has thought of a way to turn it off.

God sees everything and hears everything and is every-where which keeps him pretty busy. So you shouldn't go wasting his time by going over your mom and dad's head asking for something they said you couldn't have.

Jesus is God's Son. He used to do all the hard work like walking on water and performing miracles and trying to teach the people who didn't want to learn about God. They finally got tired of him preaching to them and they crucified Him. But He was good and kind, like His Father and He told His Father that they didn't know what they were doing and to forgive them, and God said OK.

His Dad (God) appreciated everything that He had done and all His hard work on earth so He told Him He didn't have to go out on the road anymore. He could stay in heaven. So He did. And now He helps His Dad out by listening to prayers and seeing things which are important for God to take care of and which ones He can take care of Himself without having to bother God. Like a secretary, only more important.

You can pray anytime you want and they are sure to help you because they got it worked out so one of them is on duty all the time.

If you don't believe in God, besides being an atheist, you will be very lonely, because your parents can't go everywhere with you, like to camp, but God can. It is good to know He's around you when you're scared in the dark or when you can't swim and you get thrown into real deep water by big kids.

But . . . you shouldn't just always think of what God can do for you. I figure God put me here and He can take me back anytime He pleases. And . . . that's why I believe in God.

AN EIGHT-YEAR-OLD
in response to a homework assignment:
"Explain God"

Where Is the Perfection?

In Brooklyn, New York, Chush is a school that caters to learning-disabled children. At a Chush fund-raising dinner, the father of one of the children delivered a speech that would never be forgotten by all who attended. After extolling the school for its dedicated staff, he cried out, "Where is the perfection in my son, Shaya? Everything God does is done with perfection. But my child cannot understand things as other children do. My child cannot remember facts and figures as other children do. Where is God's perfection?"

The audience was shocked by the question, pained by the father's anguish, and stilled by the piercing query.

"I believe," the father answered, "that when God brings a child like this into the world, the perfection he seeks is in the way people react to this child."

He then told the following story about his son, Shaya:

One afternoon, Shaya and his father walked past a park where some boys Shaya knew were playing baseball. The boy asked his father, "Do you think they will let me play?"

The father knew that his son was not athletic and that most boys would not want him on their team. But he also understood that if his son was chosen to play, it would give him a comfortable sense of belonging. Shaya's father approached one of the boys in the field and asked if Shaya could play.

The boy looked around for guidance from his teammates. Getting none, he took matters into his own hands and said, "We are losing by six runs and the game is in the eighth inning. I guess he can be on our team and we'll try to put him up to bat in the ninth inning."

Shaya's father was ecstatic as his son smiled broadly. Shaya was told to put on a glove and go out to play short-center field. In the bottom of the eighth inning, his team scored a few runs but was still behind by three. At the bottom of the ninth, they scored again, and now—with two outs and bases loaded—the potential winning run was on base. Shaya was scheduled to be up. Would the team actually let him bat at this juncture and give away their chance to win the game?

Surprisingly, Shaya was given the bat. Everyone knew that it was all but impossible because he didn't even know how to hold the bat properly, let alone hit with it. However, as he stepped up to the plate, the pitcher moved a few steps to lob the ball in softly, so the boy could at least be able to make contact. The first pitch came. Shaya swung clumsily and missed. One of his teammates came up to him and together they held the bat and faced the pitcher waiting for the next pitch.

The pitcher again took a few steps forward to toss the ball softly toward Shaya. As the pitch came in, he and his teammate swung at the ball, and together they hit a slow ground ball to the pitcher. The pitcher picked up the grounder and could easily have thrown it to the first baseman. Shaya would have been out, and that would have ended the game.

Instead, the pitcher threw the ball on a high arc to right field, far beyond the reach of the first baseman. Everyone started yelling, "Shaya, run to first! Run to first!"

Never in his life had Shaya "run to first." He scampered down the baseline, wide-eyed and startled. By the time he reached the base, the right fielder had the ball. He could have thrown it to the second baseman who would tag out Shaya, who was still running. But the right fielder understood the pitcher's intentions, so he threw the ball high and far over the third baseman's head.

Everyone yelled, "Run to second; run to second!"

Shaya ran toward second base as the runners ahead of him deliriously circled the bases toward home.

As he reached second base, the opposing shortstop ran to him, turned him in the direction of third base and shouted, "Run to third!"

As Shaya rounded third, the boys from both teams ran behind him screaming, "Run home!"

Shaya ran home and stepped on home plate. All eighteen boys lifted him on their shoulders and made him the hero, as he had just hit a grand slam and won the game for his team.

"That day," the father said softly with tears now running down his face, "those eighteen boys reached their level of God's perfection."

AUTHOR UNKNOWN

The First Pancake

A mother was preparing pancakes for her sons, Kevin, five, and Ryan, three. The boys began to argue over who would get the first pancake. Their mother saw the opportunity for a moral lesson. "If Jesus were sitting here, He would say, 'Let my brother have the first pancake. I can wait.'"

Kevin turned to his younger brother and said, "Ryan, you be Jesus."

AUTHOR UNKNOWN

The Price of One Hour

A man came home from work late again, tired and irritated, to find his five-year-old son waiting for him at the door.

"Daddy, may I ask you a question?"

"Sure, what is it?" replied the man.

"Daddy, how much money do you make an hour?"

"That's none of your business. What makes you ask such a thing?" the man said angrily.

"I just want to know. Please tell me, how much you make an hour?" pleaded the boy.

"If you must know, I make twenty dollars an hour."

"Oh," the little boy replied, head bowed. Then, looking up, he said, "Daddy, may I borrow ten dollars please?"

The father was furious. "If the only reason you wanted to know how much money I make is just so you can borrow some to buy a silly toy or some other nonsense, then you march yourself straight to your room and go to bed. Think about why you're being so selfish. I work long, hard hours everyday and don't have time for such childish games."

The boy quietly went to his room and shut the door. His father sat down and started to get even madder about the boy's questioning. How dare he ask such questions only to get some money!

After an hour or so, the man had calmed down and started to think he may have been a little hard on his son. Maybe there was something he really needed to buy with that ten dollars, and he didn't ask for money very often. The man went to the door of his son's room and opened it.

"Are you asleep, son?" he asked.

"No, Daddy, I'm awake."

"I've been thinking. Maybe I was too hard on you earlier. . . . It's been a long day and I took my aggravation out on you. Here's that ten dollars you asked for."

The little boy sat straight up, beaming.

"Oh, thank you, Daddy," he yelled. Then, reaching under his pillow, he pulled out some more crumpled-up bills.

The man, seeing that the boy already had money, started to get angry again.

The little boy slowly counted out his money, then looked up at his father.

"Why did you want more money if you already had some?" the father grumbled.

"Because I didn't have enough, but now I do," the boy explained. "Daddy, I have twenty dollars now. Can I buy an hour of your time?"

AUTHOR UNKNOWN

Priceless Art

A kindergarten teacher was observing her classroom of children while they drew. She would occasionally walk around to see each child's artwork. As she got to one little girl who was working diligently, she asked what the drawing was. The girl replied, "I'm drawing God."

The teacher paused and said, "But no one knows what God looks like." Without missing a beat or looking up from her drawing, the girl replied, "They will in a minute."

AUTHOR UNKNOWN

Amanda Bender 10 Elkhart IN

PART TWO

A Comfort
in the Darkness

Safe in the Word

Tyler, our four-year-old grandson, was anxiously waiting to sleep in his very own brand-new bedroom. He had been sharing a bedroom with his little brother, Jordan, but now each one had a new decorated room.

When his mother checked on him before retiring for the night, Tyler was still wide awake.

"Why aren't you asleep Tyler? Are you afraid of being alone?"

Tyler responded, "No, because I have Dad's little Bible and I'll be safe because Jesus' Word is with me."

This little boy had gotten his dad's New Testament out of his bedside table and had it clutched in his little hand, held up by his face.

A small child honors Jesus' word, remembering Psalm 73:23 (NRSV): "I am continually with you; you hold my right hand."

CAROLYN LOOS
Seymour, Ind.

All Night Long

"Imagine Jesus sitting in a chair right beside your bed as a loving, comforting presence, with you all night long."

This was the advice I gave two of my daughters at different times when they were having trouble sleeping.

When my eleven-year-old daughter used this advice, she told me the next morning, "It worked!"

My fifteen-year-old daughter was dealing with the tragic death of a friend who was near her own age. She was having great difficulty sleeping. She used the advice I had given and shared with me these results: "It wasn't working so I imagined He was holding my hand. That didn't quite do it either. I then imagined that He had his arms around me holding me as a comforting parent would do. Then it worked. I felt safe and secure, and was able to sleep."

My fifteen-year-old is now almost eighteen, and when I was talking with her about sharing this story, she said, "I'm not sure when I first started doing that. You might have shared that advice with me when I was younger. Anyway, I know I've been using it for a long time, and I still use it when I have trouble sleeping."

As we get older, we do not outgrow our need for God's comfort; in fact, we might need it even more. No matter what age we are, to God we are still His children and He wants to comfort us.

DEBBIE (MAHAN) RUSSELL
Frankfort, Ind.

16

Dreams in the Storm

That evening in April 1980 was no different from many others—baths, bedtime stories, and kisses—for my two daughters who were four and seven years old at the time. My husband, Lin, wasn't at home that evening to participate in the bedtime rituals. He was in the middle of a statewide campaign for attorney general of Indiana. He put thirty thousand miles on our car that year and occasionally traveled by private plane when it was too far to drive. Even though the campaign kept him away from home a lot, he always made it a priority to get home rather than stay in a motel.

That evening I didn't expect him home until very late, so I went on to bed about 11:00 P.M. For some reason Shelley, my four year old, was having a fitful night—not fully awake, but tossing, turning, and crying out in her sleep. I made several trips to the side of her bed to try to comfort her. She was talking in her sleep, but nothing seemed to make sense to me.

Each time I arose to check on her, I looked at the clock—midnight, 12:30 A.M., 1 A.M. With each passing hour I became more apprehensive. Lin was always home by midnight. Where was he at this hour?

Again, I went to Shelley's bedside in response to her cries. As I stood next to her bed rubbing her back to try to calm her, three words were intelligible: "Daddy . . . airplane . . . wet."

I was immediately alarmed because Lin was flying home from Evansville in a private plane that night—something

Shelley had no way of knowing—and a fierce storm was raging outside.

I knew without a doubt that God was speaking to me through Shelley. Lin was in trouble, and I needed to pray for him.

"Lord, somehow through Shelley, you are telling me that I need to pray for Lin. Please put your arms around him and bring him home safely."

Finally at 1:30 A.M., I heard the familiar sound of the garage door opening, and I knew he had made it home safely.

"I was so worried about you!"

"You won't believe what I've been through. Our plane nearly crashed in a violent thunderstorm," he said.

"I already knew that," I said. "Through Shelley, God awakened me to pray for your safety. 'Daddy . . . airplane . . . wet.' Those were her only words I could decipher. But they were enough that I knew you were in trouble and needed my prayers."

Shelley slept soundly the rest of the night, and the next morning she had no recollection of her dreams the night before.

We had no doubts that God, in His mysterious and miraculous ways, worked through Shelley that night. He had indeed put His arms around Lin and brought him home safely.

DIANE PEARSON
Frankfort, Ind.

White Presence

I remember a constant, loving, peaceful presence, all in white, near the right side of my bed.

When I was a child around seven years old and in second grade, I became very ill. The pediatrician that checked me diagnosed that I had hepatitis. What he missed was that I also had rheumatic fever. So, instead of getting better, I got much worse and ended up in the hospital. Later, I came to understand from what my parents told me, I was not expected to live through one of the nights.

From that time in the hospital, I remember no fear. What I do clearly remember is a constant, loving, peaceful presence. It was like a person all in white, at the right side of my bed, near my right hand. I know my parents have said they stayed with me, but I doubt they wore all white and stayed in one spot the whole time!

I definitely felt love and peace no matter what was happening to me physically. There is no doubt in my mind that what I felt was expressed and shown to me through my parents and also from beyond my parents.

Dear Abba Father, thank you for giving me love and peace, then and now, through whatever ways you choose.

DEBBIE (MAHAN) RUSSELL
Frankfort, Ind.

Breath Prayer

When my ten-year-old daughter was preparing herself for a difficult hospital stay, my brother Ken shared a powerful idea with her—the technique of using breath prayers. He said, "As you breathe in (inhale), think Dear God, or Dear Abba, or Holy Spirit, or Father, whatever you feel comfortable calling God. As you breathe out (exhale), think of a brief phrase (two, three, or four words) stating your deepest need; for example, give me peace, give me love, help me forgive, help me love."

She said she knew instantly what her breath prayer would be: "Dear God, help me do this."

From her hospital window she could see a light at night. She said, "It was only a streetlight, but when I prayed and looked at the light in the darkness outside my window, it helped me feel that God was near and that I wasn't alone."

Looking to the light, she used her breath prayer. As she faced her tough situation, she used her breath prayer over and over. She went through that struggle, overcame it, and her faith grew in the process.

She said to me, "God answered my prayers. It feels so wonderful to experience that! It really works. He helped me."

My brother, in my opinion, had thrown her a lifeline and encouraged her to grab hold and hang on!

Take time to encourage and to share with others what has helped you in your faith journey. It just may be part of what helps another person get connected and stay connected through their time of struggle.

God is the light and He is with us through it all. God is aware of our every breath!

DEBBIE (MAHAN) RUSSELL
Frankfort, Ind.

Standin' in the Need of Prayer

One Sunday in a Midwest city, a young child was acting up during the morning worship hour. The parents did their best to maintain some sense of order in the pew but were losing the battle. Finally the father picked the little fellow up and walked sternly up the aisle on his way out. Just before reaching the foyer, the little one called loudly to the congregation, "Pray for me! Pray for me!"

AUTHOR UNKNOWN

PART THREE

Ministers of
All Sizes

Glue for the Little Pieces

"What's wrong, Mommy?"

I said, "I feel like I'm falling apart in little pieces, but I'll be all right after awhile."

Then my 3-year-old daughter, Jessica, said with confidence, "I'll glue you back together."

Wow! How could I help but smile. My little daughter ministered to me in that moment.

All this happened some years ago. Jessica is now almost eighteen, and I still remember that moment clearly because she touched my heart.

On that day, stress had built up to the point I just needed to cry. I was in the kitchen, cleaning up some dishes, when Jessica walked in. I just kept washing dishes hoping she wouldn't notice my tears. She noticed. Even at her young age, she wanted to help when she realized I felt troubled.

Jessica was not too young, and we are not too old to reach out in support and love.

"I'll glue you back together." Isn't that what God does for us? He heals our brokenness and makes us whole through the gift of His grace—the glue that holds us together!

DEBBIE (MAHAN) RUSSELL
Frankfort, Ind.

Matthew Paul, the Minister

Matthew Paul is a loveable, smiling Down's syndrome child who was born with several physical ailments. Early in his young life he was hospitalized with several serious surgeries. During those hospitalizations, he and his family became very close to Pastor B, their home church minister.

Matthew Paul's family brought him to church as an infant, and he seemed to really enjoy being there. The music was always the part of worship he liked best—as long as it wasn't too loud! From an early age, he would recognize and high-five Pastor B. It wasn't too long before he would get excited and run into Pastor B's arms when he saw him at a distance.

In his church, the children's message was about ten minutes after worship began. Matthew Paul was always one of the first to find a perch down front, and he listened attentively to the special words for his age group. After the message, the children were dismissed for Sunday School. Sometimes Matthew Paul preferred to sit with his parents in the pew rather than exit with his older brother Christopher.

One Sunday, the summer before Matthew Paul started a regular kindergarten class, he decided to sit in the pew in front of his parents after the children's message. Cautiously they agreed, sitting forward in their seats to make sure his actions did not get out of control.

He began to copy Pastor B's hand gestures. When Pastor B raised his hands to emphasize a point in his sermon, Matthew Paul raised his right hand. When Pastor B stood up or sat down, Matthew Paul copied the same action. When Pastor B clapped his hands together to draw attention to a point, the boy clapped his hands. At the end of the service, he followed Pastor B out after the benediction. There he proceeded to greet the congregation by shaking each person's hand as they left. One of the parishioner's exclaimed: "Matthew Paul's going to grow up to be a minister, just like Pastor B."

Matthew Paul is loved by old and young alike in that congregation. It was in that church family where he felt acceptance and encouragement to be an active participant in worship. That acceptance has spilled over to the community where he is an active T-ball and soccer player as well as a favorite in the local elementary school.

HEATHER OLSON-BUNNELL
Decatur, Ind.

Kevin Bender Age 11 Elkhart IN

A Piece of Cake and a Prayer

When I first met Victoria, I was astonished by the brightness in her deep, blue eyes. This child loved to play, like any other child of three, and wanted her grandmother to help her in that play. She was curious about the world around her and interested in touching and experimenting.

Victoria seemed to me to be a typical young child. However, I soon realized that at three years old, she was, indeed, anything but typical. She was a miracle child. She had already conquered the doctors' warnings that she would only have a 20 percent chance of survival.

But, at nearly four, the family was once more facing the ravages of the dreaded illness we call cancer. Not only had the same cancer reappeared, but a new, unknown cancer, was present. This time the doctors wouldn't even give Victoria a 20 percent chance. But in spite of what we know in modern medicine, faith remained evident.

On her fourth birthday, the family gathered in her hospital room in Indianapolis to share the celebration of her birth. As her grandmother relayed the experience to me, she was "somewhat surprised to see that it was Victoria who was concerned that each person in the room had a piece of cake, a fork, and a napkin. It was also Victoria who would not let anyone eat that piece of cake until they had all gathered together, held hands, and said a prayer. A prayer which Victoria led in her sweet, young way." A miracle child—only as we humans view her medically—Victoria is a child of God, now and forever!

DOROTHY DEXHEIMER
Kokomo, Ind.

Beyond Expectations

Sarah, age twelve, attended South Indiana Special Needs Camp in 1997 and 1998. Because Sarah has cerebral palsy, she uses a motorized wheelchair and needs helping hands when she eats and dresses.

In a voice wispy as a zephyr, Sarah directed our every facilitating act. She instructed teen counselors when they recharged her chair's battery, squirted mustard on her hotdog, and slipped the sartorially correct stretchy hair bow around her Pebbles-like topknot.

On the morning of the second day at camp, we set out for a two-mile hike. Sarah was keen to explore the trails winding deep into the woods. Hindered by crisscrossing tree roots and sharp rain-washed inclines, we switched her wheelchair to manual drive. With ropes, a team of counselors eased Sarah and her chair to our destination, a creek that runs along the north end of the campground.

I lifted Sarah from her chair and handed her to a young counselor who was seated near where the water falls into a shallow stone-bottom pool.

"I want to put my feet into the water," Sarah said. We removed her tiny sandals and socks, and the counselor shifted Sarah so that her feet—tender as a baby's—dipped into the swirling pool just below the falls.

Sarah's eyes and grin widened in surprised pleasure. "A creek is much colder than I had expected," she said. Sarah delights in experiences that prove more than she expects.

We would eat our lunch beside the trickling waterfall, but first we had our Bible lesson: the "loving of your enemies" teaching from Luke's Gospel. We discussed the message. Sarah raised her hand. Her arm was so narrow that her pink WWJD ("What Would Jesus Do?") bracelet dropped nearly to her elbow.

"Actually," she said. Sarah often begins a response with "actually," hinting that the answer comes from introspection and deliberation. "Actually, I'm only in middle school, and I've had little chance to make enemies." She paused for a breath. "But some people act like I'm not really there."

Ah yes, I thought, our worst enemies don't challenge us; they wish us away. For the moment, I put myself inside the slight body of Sarah. How easy for a hard-hearted person to wish her away—a piece of cake.

"I pray for them," she said. Her cheeks pinked, flushed with an awareness of her show of strength.

I am thankful for children like Sarah who are delighted when life is more than they expect, who wear WWJD bracelets, and ponder ways to love their enemies.

And I am thankful for parents like Sarah's who put on brave smiles and allow experiences beyond expectations, and who trust Jesus' teachings will be the sufficient safeguard for their precious children.

ANNE HOLTSCLAW MEYER
Indianapolis, Ind.

Seeing Invisible

When two of my daughters were very young, they were looking out of the sliding glass door to our backyard and the school yard beyond that. My four-year-old daughter, Rachel, saw some large, unusual birds. She asked her two-year-old sister Laura, "Do you see them out there?"

Laura was looking, but not seeing what Rachel was talking about.

"Do you see them out there?" Rachel asked again.

Laura still didn't see them.

Then Rachel said, "Well honey, they're invisible. I see invisible."

Laura, being only two, accepted that explanation; and maybe Rachel at that young age, thought she might be able to see something invisible, because she knew what she saw but her sister couldn't see it. When Laura turned three years old, we discovered she needed glasses.

"See those birds out there? I see invisible." Do we see what some others do not? Do we see the invisible spirit at work within ourselves and others? Possibly we may need special glasses and not know it! We may be missing a deeper sight. Maybe we need some help for our vision to open up.

Listen and search and look with your heart. The invisible, abundant spirit of God is within us.

DEBBIE (MAHAN) RUSSELL
Frankfort, Ind.

All the White Apples

A friend's son was in the first grade of school, and his teacher asked the class, "What is the color of apples?" Most of the children answered red. A few said green. Kevin, my friend's son, raised his hand and said white. The teacher tried to explain that apples could be red, green, or sometimes golden but never white.

Kevin was quite insistent and finally said, "Look inside."

Perception without mindfulness keeps us on the surface of things, and we often miss other levels of reality.

JOSEPH GOLDSTEIN
Insight Meditation

Of Life, Death, and Dogs

Some of the most poignant moments I spend as a veterinarian are those spent with my clients assisting the transition of my animal patients from this world to the next. When living becomes a burden, whether from pain or loss of normal functions, I can help a family by ensuring that their beloved pet has an easy passing. Making this final decision is painful, and I have often felt powerless to comfort the grieving owners.

That was before I met Shane. I had been called to examine a ten-year-old blue heeler named Belker who had developed a serious health problem. The dog's owners—Ron, his wife, Lisa, and their little boy, Shane—were all very attached to Belker and they were hoping for a miracle. I examined Belker and found he was dying of cancer. I told the family there were no miracles left for Belker, and offered to perform the euthanasia procedure for the old dog in their home. As we made arrangements, Ron and Lisa told me they thought it would be good for the four-year-old Shane to observe the procedure. They felt Shane could learn something from the experience.

The next day, I felt the familiar catch in my throat as Belker's family surrounded him. Shane seemed so calm, petting the old dog for the last time, that I wondered if he understood what was going on. Within a few minutes, Belker slipped peacefully away. The little boy seemed to accept Belker's transition without any difficulty or confusion. We sat together for a while after Belker's death, wondering aloud about the sad fact that animal lives are shorter than human lives. Shane, who had been listening quietly, piped up, "I know why." Startled, we all turned to him. What came out of his mouth next stunned me—I'd never heard a more comforting explanation.

He said, "Everybody is born so that they can learn how to live a good life—like loving everybody and being nice, right?" The four-year-old continued, "Well, animals already know how to do that, so they don't have to stay as long."

AUTHOR UNKNOWN

Ryan's Call

Ryan has red hair and an award-winning smile. He was ten years old and in the fifth grade the day he came to my office. He had called me on the phone and made an appointment—so I knew it was serious business!

The first words out of his mouth were:

"Pastor Heather, God is telling me to preach a sermon. He has some things He wants me to say in worship."

One of the great things about being a pastor to children is their openness to God's call in their lives. They are usually eager to tell you about it. That day I told my secretary to hold my calls as Ryan and I explored exactly what God was calling him to say. It was a powerful message—about forgiveness.

There was no question in my mind that this was from God. Ryan shared his concerns about first writing the message. I was impressed that he realized he needed to write the text down. That morning we opened the Bible together and listed some passages on forgiveness for him to research. We made an appointment for him to come back to discuss the actual writing of the message.

Then I went to the senior pastor and raised Ryan's request. I had started a Saturday evening worship service there with an average attendance of fifty to sixty people. I suggested we invite children to lead one entire service—read the Scripture, write a prayer, perform special music, etc. and have Ryan bring the message that God was telling him to share. We were off and running!

Ryan's rough draft was excellent. His mother later told me he worked at his desk for over ten hours on it and wouldn't let her see it!

That Saturday night over one hundred persons, including some of the teachers at Ryan's school, were in attendance. He placed his notes on the pulpit, then imitated my preaching style, by coming forward and beginning his message without them.

Ryan shared how he once broke his mother's favorite flower vase and his mother's face "turned as red as spaghetti sauce," but she put her loving arms around him and told him it was okay. She forgave him. Ryan shared how God's love was like that—always forgiving, forgetting, and moving on. Ryan went on to say that that was the model we should follow in our relationships with others.

As I hugged Ryan after his message, I knew deep in my heart that God was really using him to reach others in the congregation that night.

HEATHER OLSON-BUNNELL
Roanoke, Ind.

PART FOUR

Grace
Remembered

Trusting as a Child

God says that we must be as children. I feel like a child: I talk to him quite a bit. It seems that amidst the conversations, there are answers—if I listen. I learned, for instance, that I can have good things happen to me. I learned, too, that I can have peace among the storms.

Just as I was enjoying a bit of calmness in my life, my daughter explained that she was pregnant again. For most people, this would be a thrill and a half. But, having had the experience of one premature baby, I wasn't celebrating this one. At sixteen weeks gestation, the doctor performed a procedure on my daughter, Tanya, to keep the baby from moving further into the birth canal. This didn't work; so, like many mothers in her position, my daughter was not allowed to get out of bed until she went into labor.

Nine weeks later, at twenty-five weeks, she gave birth to a one pound, eight-ounce baby girl. I couldn't imagine that we would be lucky enough to have another preemie come home without major problems—or even alive. They named her Kelsey. Her lung collapsed, followed by numerous other crises. After she was brought home, she developed whooping cough, and she stopped breathing in my arms. She recovered.

"Well, God, how long could we have her for?" I wondered.

Yet, God saved this bundle of joy. When I would pray, I would say, "I understand why you wouldn't save her, but can't you anyway?" Not a great prayer for someone who claims to be a great believer. It has taken three years for me to believe that we wouldn't lose her. She is a smart, analytical little imp with a big mouth. God is teaching me to trust. He's teaching me to have faith in His love and wisdom. He's teaching me about His omnipotence. All I can do is praise Him and keep my heart open to His lessons.

P.S. When my first preemie grandbaby was in the incubator, I would sing, "Jesus loves you," to him. I also sang "Jesus loves me." Last week, this five-year-old grandson looked at me and said, "Grandma, do you know that Jesus loves me? He loves you, too . . . and Kelsey." What a reminder of God's greatness!

ELAINE DASH

Hobart, Ind.

When Nothing Else Could Help

I had all but given up on my battle with an uncontrollable temper. There had been fights at school and verbal outbursts against my brothers and sisters. Some stubborn arguments were directed at my parents. At the age of seven, or maybe eight, I was a mess of fears and rage.

One of my duties on the farm was to split firewood into thin pieces for the kitchen stove. Leaning a piece to be split against the splitting log, I swung the axe. The piece not only split but also broke into short missiles which flew up with great wrath and struck me in the forehead. I really wasn't injured but my temper flared into rage. I threw the axe at the [censored] pieces of wood and cussed them out with all of the words learned from men who used such embellishments when they were vexed or wanted to impress their peers.

At the end of my tirade I heard a familiar voice. I shall never forget that moment. My mother had simply spoken my name. Standing there just a few feet away on the other side of the fence, she had seen and heard the whole episode. With love she had spoken my name. Then in a calm voice she asked if I would do something for her. Boy, would I ever! Anything! I was caught. Man was I caught! So I said, "Yes." And she said, "When you feel that way, would you just say three little words, 'Jesus help me,' and then look up and try to smile."

I said "OK," and walked off around the corner of the woodshed, muttering as I walked. "Of all the dumb sissy . . . Jesus help me . . . Look up and smile . . . grumble . . . grumble!"

Somehow as I walked and fumed, I halfway began doing what she had suggested. And there in the middle of the barn lot, stopped in my tracks—it dawned on me: this stuff works; it really works! Something wonderful is going on. And so began an experiment with prayer. So began a life journey of deepening relationships with God and with people. Where once were fear and rage came quiet confidence. Where once was contention is now peace and harmony. All because of genuine love wisely given to a messed-up boy on a farm in southern Indiana.

Every time I recall that signal event in my life, an old song comes to mind and touches my soul: "Love lifted me, love lifted me. When nothing else could help, love lifted me!"

CHESTER A. MAHAN
Boyne Falls, Mich.

Joannie Remembered

When mothers or fathers say they don't take their children to Sunday school because they want their children to decide for themselves what they want to believe, my heart breaks.

This decision sends my mind on a roller-coaster ride into the parenting mind of make believe. I picture children with moldy teeth because their parents don't want to upset them in case they don't like the taste of the toothpaste, or visiting dentists. Do the parents not teach the children about finances because the little ones can't count? Do the parents not feed them vegetables because they don't know what the foods taste like and the children hear from other children that "veggies taste nasty"?

In church and Sunday School, I watch children—who only get the type of attention that comes with misbehavior—listen attentively to stories of Jesus. I watch them play the games where no one "dies," and make rules where it's okay to lose or make mistakes.

I listen to their little voices say, "Jesus loves me" with a little less stress in their eyes—even if it's only for a moment.

I was listening to a woman named Joannie, who was fighting single-handedly to pick herself and her children up from physical and mental abuse. I wondered what gave her such fight.

I wondered if she believed in God.

One day, while we were talking, I asked her if she went to church. While we spoke, she told me of a memory of her childhood. She said when times were really bad and her husband told her she was worthless, she remembered the times that her Sunday school teacher smiled at her, hugged her, and watched over her as she headed home. Sometimes this teacher would call on her during the week. (Her home life as a child was kind of like her sad married life.)

When Joannie remembered this Sunday school teacher's love, which was Christ's love, she could believe in God. She knew she was worth something—to God. So she knew that she was fighting for something important. Despite a life of negativity, she had learned from a Sunday school teacher that she was important. One faithful person brought enough love into her life when she was a child to give her the fight to go on in her adversity as an adult.

ELAINE DASH
Hobart, Ind.

From a Child's Blossoming Belief

I received the call from school—"Your daughter is sick and needs to come home." This was about the umpteenth time since I don't know when. Lynn had a headache again. I was at work and needed to be home, but I was hoping my work record would not be jeopardized. So far they had understood. It seemed like once we got home and Lynn took a nap, she felt better. I was beginning to think she was just tired and wanted to come home; she always did need more sleep than most children her age.

Once I got to school, I realized she was truly sick—her eyes had that glassy look about them and you could just see the pain in her face. She was a trooper though. All she would say is, "My head hurts so bad." We would go home and after a nap, she would begin feeling better. The doctors put her through a battery of tests to no avail. There were brain scans to check for a brain tumor. She had an EEG, an MRI, and tons of medications in an effort to knock out these headaches. At one time she was put on an adult dose of medication since the children's strength didn't help. This medication overdosed her and landed her in the hospital. My heart would go out to her, and I felt so bad since I could not make her feel better.

She and her sister both attended Sunday School on a regular basis along with going to church as a family. I don't know if she understood the concept of prayer totally since she was only in elementary school. We always tried to pray at meals and I know she prayed at Sunday School. I truly feel God touched her heart one time during one of her headache bouts. As she was lying on the bed in pain, she looked up at me and said, "Mommy, I'm not afraid to die." I realized she knew what could relieve her of her pain.

As she grew older, Lynn was very active in her youth group. She and her sister, Tina, approached our minister at the time and requested a new type of group—one that would study the Bible more and be more serious. Our minister was very receptive to the idea and revamped the group. She stayed active in the group and went to many retreats and attended many learning camps. As the Lord continued to work within her, she approached our minister once again to help her deal with some issues. I never did know what they were or the reason, but she grew up and graduated from Taylor University with a degree in youth ministry. After being our youth and education director for many years, she quit to start a family.

Lynn and her husband Scott now have two beautiful girls, Hannah and Chauncea. I know she still has the Spirit in her soul. Hannah is only two and she knows what it is to pray. Lynn and Hannah prayed one time in the doctor's office when Hannah was upset. Returning to the same doctor about one month later, Hannah wanted to pray as soon as they stopped in the parking lot. God is working in that little soul—hopefully, one day she will grow up just like her mother and be a beacon for Christ.

MARY LOU PARKER
Montmorenci, Ind.

December Butterflies

My niece Stephanie's life was but twenty years long. Today she would have been twenty-four.

Remembering Stephanie is like recalling the butterflies of last summer. Quietly, gracefully, she brightened God's world. A friend once described her: "Delicate, beautiful, sensitive, and fun to admire, Stephanie and butterflies seem to make everything they touch just that much more spectacular." The friend that compared Stephanie to a perfect butterfly has a daughter whose birthday is the exact day that Stephanie died in the accident. He said that he will continue to use Stephanie as a role model for his daughter. Many, many others will, also.

In her high school's salutatorian speech, my niece said that life resembled four things:

Keys—to many doors of opportunities. Some joyful and others disappointing.

Rubber bands—symbolizing our need to stretch our minds and bodies to be in shape for future problems. Remain flexible. If snapped, you become useless.

A ball of clay waiting to be molded—It's up to you (with God's help) to shape it and form it into what you envision your life to be. Use your talents and skills to make your life a work of art.

And a candle—she quoted George Bernard Shaw. "Life is no brief candle to me, it is a sort of splendid torch which I have got hold of for the moment, and I want to make it burn as brightly as possible before handing it on to the future generations."

Stephanie gained much wisdom in her short stay here on earth. Her relationship with Jesus was evident.

Jesus' life was approximately thirty years long. Nearly two thousand years later, the torch He carried in His spirit continues to burn as an example of how we should live our lives. It is exceptional that so much came forth from such a brief life.

The same can be said of butterflies and others, perhaps, who have birthdays in December.

TERESA WITKOSKE
Wabash, Ind.

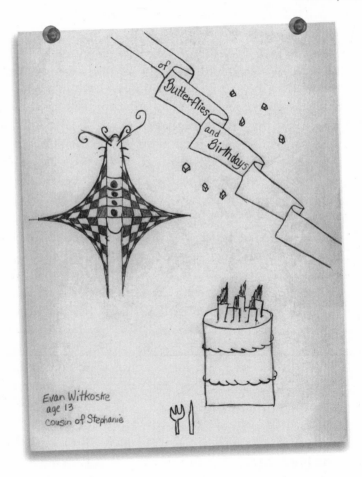

Evan Witkoske
age 13
Cousin of Stephanie

No Deals with God

My daughter was in her twenty-seventh week of pregnancy when I received the disturbing call from her. She was in labor—three months early. In a stupor, I found myself barreling down the expressway with emergency lights blinking and horn blowing. The stormy evening seemed to reflect my stormy emotions. A short time after I arrived, she gave birth to a blue two-pound baby boy. The specialists worked on the still body in the delivery room.

Round one: he made it up to the small neonatal unit. Hope. They performed a procedure that allowed air to be pumped into his small lungs. This procedure is called "bagging." I watched. Each time he stabilized, I would walk down to my daughter's room. By the time I returned, that precious baby was being "bagged" again. Each time he stabilized, I would walk down the hall. By the time I returned to him, he was in crisis. It seemed as long as I stayed with him, he would stay stabilized. I felt as if there was an invisible string connecting us, as if I were breathing for him. I asked God to take my breath—my lungs even, but let him live. I made an agreement that God could have my lungs or my life, if he would just let my grandbaby live. Kyle did live. He is a constant joy. But the story goes on.

Two years after we brought him home, I developed a cold, then bronchitis. After an X ray, the doctor called with the news that I had a spot on my lung and needed some follow-up tests. I went through the usual fears and sorrows. Then, the "agreement" popped back into my mind. God held up His part of the bargain. I had to do the same. I thanked him for the healthy baby playing in the other room, then set up the tests. Strangely, when I completed the test, they sent me for another, then another. I just knew I only had hours to live. Instead, a perplexed nurse explained that they couldn't find any sign of the "spot."

It was a few days later that I realized what a wonderful gift I had been given.

God showed me that he doesn't make deals. He gave us Kyle, and he did it because it was meant to be.

ELAINE DASH
Hobart, Ind.

Saying Grace

A family invited some people to dinner. At the table, the mother turned to her six-year-old daughter and said, "Would you like to say the blessing?"

"I wouldn't know what to say," the girl replied.

"Just say what you hear Mommy say," the woman answered.

The daughter bowed her head and said, "Lord, why on earth did I invite all these people to dinner?"

AUTHOR UNKNOWN

Angels in the Classroom

Last school year, a teacher had a class of third graders who were either undernourished, uncared for, beaten, bruised, or raped by other family members. Her heart bled for these kids.

Before the school year started, she and her husband went to her classroom and prayed over each desk in the room. They prayed that God would place an angel behind every child to watch over them and protect them.

A month after the year had started, she asked the kids to write about what they would like to be when they grew up. Everybody was busy writing when "Andrew" raised his hand and asked how to spell "mighty." After telling him how to spell the word, she asked him why he needed to know. Andrew said it was because when he grew up, he wanted to be a "mighty man of God." When he said this, little "Mark" sitting next to him asked, "So, what's a mighty man of God?" The teacher, swallowing back her tears, and knowing she could not say anything in the classroom, told Andrew to go ahead and tell Mark what it was.

So Andrew said, "It's a man who puts on the armor of God and is a soldier for God." The teacher, with a lump in her throat, started to walk away when Andrew motioned with his forefinger for her to come closer. He whispered to her, asking if she believed in angels. She told him yes, she did. Then he asked her if she thought people could see angels, and she said she thought some people probably could. Andrew said that he did, and he could see an angel standing behind each kid in the room. . . .

AUTHOR UNKNOWN

Grandpa Goes to Heaven

After Grandma passed away, Grandpa came to live with Jimmy and his parents. Grandpa and little Jimmy became very close during the few years he lived there, then Grandpa also passed away.

After Grandpa's death, Jimmy became very worried, because he wasn't sure whether Grandpa had really gone to heaven. Although Jimmy and his family went to church every Sunday, Grandpa hadn't always gone along. Jimmy lost his appetite—he wasn't eating well or sleeping well either. His parents were becoming worried about him.

Then one night, after he finally got to sleep, an angel came to him in a dream and said, "Jimmy, come along with me. Your Grandpa wants to see you." The angel took him to a place where there was a beautiful blue lagoon. The water was crystal clear underneath a bright blue sky. There sat Grandpa with a fishing pole by his side. Grandpa hugged his little grandson, then said, "I hear you're worried about me. Well Jimmy, I'm really in heaven, and Grandma is up here with me. You see, when I didn't go to church, I came out here because I wanted to be alone to talk to God. You can talk to God anywhere, anyplace, at anytime and he will always listen and hear you. Jimmy, you have many more years left to live before you can see me again, but I know you will be in heaven with me someday. For now, don't worry about me anymore."

Then the angel took Jimmy home. When he woke up, he went downstairs where his mother was cooking breakfast, and his father was reading the morning paper. He said, "Mother, I'm hungry!" Then he told his parents the story of how the angel took him to see Grandpa, and he knew now that Grandpa was really, truly in heaven.

KEITH KISSINGER
Columbia City, Ind.

PART FIVE

Treasures for the Poor

During the June 4, 2000, opening worship service of the Memphis Annual Conference, Bishop Kenneth Carder shared a letter describing one child's gift of love and sacrifice for the children of Africa. The letter was from Beth Capuson, staff member at St. John's United Methodist Church in Memphis. The four-year-old girl, whose earliest memories are of sexual abuse and neglect, wanted to help the "poor African children who need a home." The child, who now lives with a foster family, gave Capuson a small canister one recent Sunday.

"Miss Beth, I've brought you my stuff for those kids that need a home. I gave them all I had," she said. After the child left, Capuson opened the can and found hair clips, play money, and seven cents. After reading the letter at Annual Conference, Carder opened the small can and shook out the hair clips, play money, and seven cents into his palm. Then he carefully added the little girl's treasures to the money being brought to the altar by hundreds of other children. When the pennies, dimes, and quarters were counted that night, the children had contributed $20,283, one five-dollar bill of play money, and three barrettes.

UNITED METHODIST NEWS SERVICE ITEM

Beggars' Lunch

I was a tent mother for a group of third and fourth graders during one of our church's Marketplace Vacation Bible Schools. In this program we recreate a scene as it might have looked in first century Jerusalem to give the children a sense of what life was like then. We had various market vendors, potters, weavers, and even street "beggars."

One day as we left the synagogue following worship, "beggars" approached us asking for money. Most of the children gave "coins" they had made earlier in the week. But one boy, after observing the situation for a few minutes, ran to our family tent and came back with his lunch. Giving it to the beggars, he told them his lunch was theirs to eat.

This boy, new to our congregation, had earlier experienced years of physical and emotional abuse. He now had a loving family caring for him, and the message of Christian caring had taken root in his young heart.

JOYCE COLEMAN
Floyds Knobbs, Ind.

Surprise Effect

Matt is six months older than our eleven-year-old son, Brandon, and they are best friends. They have grown up together being neighbors since their births. Matt has a brother, Brian, one and a half years older than he. Our family has been a big influence on these two boys, taking them lots of places with us including church and church-related activities.

I wasn't sure how much or how positive our influence was until Matt went out to eat with us one evening. My husband and I, Brandon, and Matt sat down and were just about to begin eating when Matt stopped and said, "Aren't we going to pray first?" I just about fell onto the floor! So, indeed we stopped to say the blessing and then eat.

Just when you think you will never get through to whomever, the unexpected happens. Hang in there, because they do hear you and see you, and you do influence them.

SUE STANTON
W. College Corner, Ind.

Patty-Cake Epiphany

We were the only family in the restaurant with children. I sat Erik in a high chair and noticed everyone was quietly eating and talking.

Suddenly, Erik squealed with glee and said, "Hi there." He pounded his fat baby hands on the high-chair tray. His eyes were wide with excitement and his mouth was bared in a toothless grin. He wriggled and giggled with merriment.

I looked around and saw the source of his merriment. It was a man with a tattered rag of a coat, dirty, greasy, and worn. His pants were baggy with a zipper at half-mast, and his toes poked out of would-be shoes. His shirt was dirty and his hair was uncombed and unwashed.

His whiskers were too short to be called a beard and his nose was so varicose it looked like a road map.

We were too far from him to tell, but I was sure he had an odor. His hands waved and flapped on loose wrists. "Hi there, baby; hi there, big boy. I see ya, buster," the man said to Erik.

My husband and I exchanged looks, "What do we do?"

Erik continued to laugh and answer, "Hi, hi there." Everyone in the restaurant noticed and looked at us, then at the man. The old geezer was creating a nuisance with my beautiful baby.

Our meal came and the man began shouting from across the room, "Do ya know patty-cake? Do you know peek-a-boo? Hey, look, he knows peek-a-boo."

56

Nobody thought the old man was cute. He was obviously drunk. My husband and I were embarrassed. We ate in silence— all except for Erik, who was running through his repertoire for the admiring skid-row bum, who in turn, reciprocated with his cute comments. We finally got through the meal and headed for the door. My husband went to pay the check and told me to meet him in the parking lot. The old man sat poised between me and the door.

"Lord, just let me out of here before he speaks to me or Erik," I prayed. As I drew closer to the man, I turned my back trying to side-step him and avoid any air he might be breathing. As I did, Erik leaned over my arm, reaching with both arms in a baby's "pick-me-up" position.

Before I could stop him, Erik had propelled himself from my arms to the man's. Suddenly a very old smelly man and a very young baby consummated their love relationship.

Erik in an act of total trust, love, and submission laid his tiny head upon the man's ragged shoulder. The man's eyes closed, and I saw tears beneath his lashes. His aged hands—full of grime, pain, and hard labor—gently, so gently cradled my baby's bottom and stroked his back. No two beings have ever loved so deeply for so short a time.

I stood awestruck. The old man rocked and cradled Erik in his arms for a moment, and then his eyes opened and set squarely on mine. He said in a firm, commanding voice, "You take care of this baby." Somehow I managed, "I will," from a throat that contained a stone.

He pried Erik from his chest unwillingly, longingly, as though he were in pain. I received my baby, and the man said, "God bless you, ma'am, you've given me my Christmas gift."

I said nothing more than a muttered thanks. With Erik in my arms, I ran for the car. My husband was wondering why I was crying and holding Erik so tightly, and why I was saying, "My God, my God, forgive me."

I had just witnessed God's love shown through the inno-cence of a tiny child who saw no sin, who made no judgment;

a child who saw a soul, and a mother who saw a suit of clothes. I was a Christian who was blind, holding a child who was not. I felt it was God asking, "Are you willing to share your son for a moment?" when He shared His for all eternity. The ragged old man, had unwittingly reminded me. "To enter the kingdom of God we must become as little children."

Author Unknown

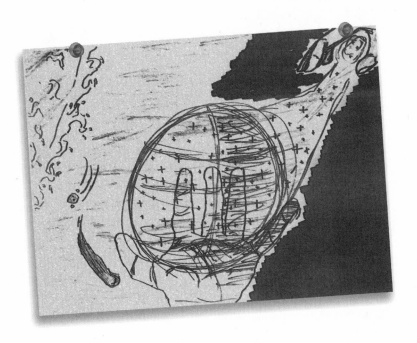

With a Pair of Shoes

An eyewitness account from New York City, on a cold day in December:

A little boy about ten years old was standing before a shoe store on the roadway, barefooted, peering through the window and shivering with cold. A lady approached the boy and said, "My little fellow, why are you looking so earnestly in that window?"

"I was asking God to give me a pair of shoes," was the boy's reply.

The lady took him by the hand and went into the store and asked the clerk to get half a dozen pairs of socks for the boy. She then asked if he could give her a basin of water and a towel. He quickly brought them to her. She took the little fellow to the back part of the store and, removing her gloves, knelt down, washed his little feet, and dried them with a towel. By this time the clerk had returned with the socks. After placing a pair of socks on the boy's feet, she purchased him a pair of shoes. Tying up the remaining pairs of socks, she gave them to him. She patted him on the head and said, "No doubt, my little fellow, you feel more comfortable now?"

As she turned to go, the astonished lad caught her by the hand, and looking up in her face, with tears in his eyes, answered the question with these words: "Are you God's wife?"

AUTHOR UNKNOWN

Fifty-seven Cents

A little girl stood crying near a small church from which she had been turned away because it "was too crowded." "I can't go to Sunday School," she sobbed to the pastor as he walked by. Seeing her shabby, unkempt appearance, the pastor guessed the reason and, taking her by the hand, went inside and found a place for her in the Sunday School class.

The child was so touched that she went to bed that night thinking of the children who have no place to worship Jesus. Some two years later, this child lay dead in one of the nearby tenement buildings, and the parents called for the pastor who had befriended their daughter to handle the final arrangements.

As her little body was being moved, a worn and crumpled purse was found which seemed to have been rummaged from some trash dump. Inside was found 57¢ and a note scribbled in childish handwriting which read, "This is to help build the little church bigger so more children can go to Sunday School."

For two years she had saved for this offering of love. When the pastor tearfully read that note, he knew instantly what he would do. Carrying the note and the cracked, red pocketbook to the pulpit, he told the story of her unselfish love. He challenged his congregation to get busy and raise enough money for the larger building. A newspaper learned of the story and published it. It was read by a realtor who offered them a parcel of land worth many thousands. When told that the church could not pay so much, he offered it for 57¢. Church members made large donations. Checks came from far and wide.

Within five years the little girl's gift had increased to $250,000—a huge sum for that time (near the turn of the century). Her love had paid large dividends. If you should visit the city of Philadelphia, visit Temple Baptist Church, with a seating capacity of thirty-three hundred and Temple University where, today, hundreds of students are trained. Have a look, too, at the Good Samaritan Hospital and at a Sunday School building which houses hundreds of Sunday scholars, so that no child in the area will ever need to be left outside during Sunday School time. In one of the rooms of this building may be seen the picture of that little girl whose 57¢, so sacrificially saved, made such remarkable history. Alongside of it is a portrait of her pastor, Dr. Russel H. Conwell.

AUTHOR UNKNOWN

PART SIX

A Brother's Sunshine

Like any good mother, when Karen found out that another baby was on the way, she did what she could to help her three-year-old son, Michael, prepare for a new sibling. They found out that the new baby was going to be a girl, and day after day, night after night, Michael sang to his sister in Mommy's tummy. The pregnancy progressed normally for Karen, an active member of the Panther Creek United Methodist Church in Morristown, Tennessee.

Then the labor pains came. Every five minutes . . . then every minute. But complications arose during delivery. Hours of labor ensued. Doctors discussed whether a C-section would be required. Finally, Michael's little sister was born, but she was in serious condition. With sirens howling in the night, the ambulance rushed the infant to the neonatal intensive care unit at St. Mary's Hospital, Knoxville, Tennessee. The days inched by. The little girl's condition worsened. The pediatric specialist told the parents, "There is very little hope. Be prepared for the worst." Karen and her husband contacted a local cemetery about a burial plot. They had fixed up a special room in their home for the new baby; now they planned a funeral.

Michael kept begging his parents to let him see his sister, "I want to sing to her," he said.

Week two in intensive care. It looked as if a funeral would come before the week was over. Michael kept nagging about singing to his sister, but kids were never allowed in intensive care. But Karen made up her mind. She would take Michael whether they liked it or not. If he didn't see his sister now, he would never see her alive.

She dressed him in an oversized scrub suit and marched him into ICU. He looked like a walking laundry basket, but the head nurse recognized him as a child and bellowed, "Get that kid out of here now! No children are allowed." The mother in Karen rose up strong, and the usually mild-mannered lady glared into the head nurse's face, her lips a firm line.

"He is not leaving until he sings to his sister!" Karen towed Michael to his sister's bedside. He gazed at the tiny infant losing the battle to live.

And he began to sing. In the pure-hearted voice of a three-year-old, Michael sang: "You are my sunshine, my only sunshine, you make me happy when skies are gray." Instantly the baby girl responded. The pulse rate became calm and steady. "Keep on singing, Michael," Karen urged.

"You never know, dear, how much I love you, Please don't take my sunshine away." The baby's ragged, strained breathing became smooth as a kitten's purr. "Keep on singing, Michael."

"The other night, dear, as I lay sleeping, I dreamed I held you in my arms . . ."

Michael's little sister relaxed as rest, healing rest, seemed to sweep over her. "Keep on singing, Michael." Tears conquered the face of the bossy head nurse. Karen glowed. "You are my sunshine, my only sunshine. Please don't take my sunshine away," he sang on.

Funeral plans were scrapped. The next day—the very next day—the little girl was well enough to go home! *Woman's Day* magazine called it "the miracle of a brother's song." The medical staff just called it a miracle. Karen called it a miracle of God's love!

AUTHOR UNKNOWN

Beverly's Song

In the first church I served, there was a little seven-year-old girl who had Down's syndrome. Her parents brought her to church school every week. At that church the first worship hour and church school were the same hour. Once a month all the children would gather in the sanctuary for the first fifteen minutes of worship and participate in a children's sermon. Then they would be dismissed to their regular Sunday School classes.

Beverly usually was kept apart from this gathering time and remained in the pew with her parents. Her occasional outbursts embarrassed her parents and they were afraid the rest of the congregation would view this as "disruptive." I encouraged them to bring her to as many events in the church as they could, since she so enjoyed being with the other children. Beverly loved to sing at the church school gathering time. She enjoyed the class activities, although she did occasionally try to eat the crayons. Her smile was contagious, and her teachers took special care to include her in all the room projects.

One Sunday, after the singing time at the start of church school, Beverly was missing. Her teachers panicked. They came to me and said, "We can't find her anywhere downstairs, where could she be?" Trying hard not to panic myself, I told them to continue the search on the lower level, and I would look upstairs. As I climbed the stairs, the director of music was looking for me. Beverly had found an open door and was standing in the empty choir loft with a hymnal open, quietly singing:

I am the church
You are the church
We are the church together.

It was prayer time. The senior pastor was unaware of the drama unfolding at the front of the sanctuary as he continued his prayer. Most of the congregation had their heads bent, although a few smiles could be seen from the opened-eyed prayers.

I coaxed Beverly out, but the tears were running down my face as well as the cheeks of the organist who started to accompany her as she sang. This little cherub had absorbed more from the corporate worship experience than any of us had ever imagined to be possible with her level of learning. In those fifteen minutes of worship once a month, Beverly was reached by God and responded back to God. *All* God's children belong in worship so the gospel call be modeled for them.

HEATHER OLSON-BUNNELL
Decatur, Ind.

Taking a Brat to the Throne

I am a teacher of students with mild disabilities. I love the challenge, but there are some days when the lack of motivation of my students really gets to me. I had recently read in one of Barbara Johnson's books about visualizing taking your child to the throne of the Lord and handing your child over to the Lord.

One day I was driving home after an especially grueling day at work. I was steaming over one particular student, and the thought of taking her to the Lord entered my mind. I visualized going up steep stairs, dragging this bratty young lady by the hands and throwing her at the feet of Jesus. He scooped her up and cradled her in his arms. She did her aggravating, high-pitched giggle, and he was rocking and laughing too! I stood there, tight-lipped, arms crossed, and boiling inside.

"You want to know what she did?" I mentally said to Jesus. "Well, she . . . she sat there and wouldn't do her work! I told her I'd give her detention and she said, 'I don't care!' She also flirts with the boys—rubs up against them, bats her big brown eyes at them. She also cries about everything and, well, she's just plain dumb! There I said it!"

Jesus looked at her with pure love in his eyes.

I said, "Well, what do you think we should do?"

He looked lovingly at me and said, "Janet, are you casting stones?"

Embarrassed, I whined, "Well Lord, I'm the one who has to be with her all day, and I'm tired of working so hard, and she doesn't appreciate it."

"Do you only want to do my work if you get recognized?" He said.

I thought for a moment and remembered my true heart's desire, "No Lord, I only want to serve you, no matter what. The results are up to you. But darn! It's so frustrating to try so hard, and they just simply refuse to do what's best for them!"

"I know, believe me. But I have given all my children the freedom to choose. And even when the choice hurts, I don't give up on them."

Humbled, I asked, "Lord, what do you want me to do?"

"Go back and try again. Remember, I promise to always be with you, and (giving the girl a squeeze) I'm with her too."

"OK," I said, reaching to take her hand.

Together she and I descended the stairs, ready to try again.

JANET L. JACKSON
Greensburg, Ind.

Ice Cream for the Soul

Last week I took my children to a restaurant. My six-year-old son had asked if he could say grace. As we bowed our heads, he said, "God is good. God is great. Thank you for the food and I will even thank you more if Mom gets us ice cream for dessert. And liberty and justice for all. Amen."

Along with the laughter from the other customers nearby, I heard a woman remark, "That's what's wrong with this country. Kids today don't even know how to pray. Asking God for ice cream. . . . Why, I never!"

Hearing this, my son burst into tears and asked me, "Did I do it wrong? Is God mad at me?" As I held him and assured him that he had done a terrific job, and God was certainly not mad at him, an elderly gentleman approached the table. He winked at my son and said, "I happen to know that God thought that was a great prayer."

"Really?" my son asked.

Then in a theatrical whisper the gentleman added (indicating the woman whose remark had started this whole thing), "Too bad she never asks God for ice cream. A little ice cream can be good for the soul."

Naturally, I bought my kids ice cream at the end of the meal. My son stared at his for a moment, then did something I will remember for the rest of my life. He picked up his sundae and—without a word—walked over and placed it in front of the woman. With a big smile he told her, "Here, this is for you. Ice cream is good for the soul sometimes, and my soul is good already."

AUTHOR UNKNOWN

All the Same, and Not

There is an old Hasidic story about a child of a rabbi who used to wander in the woods. At first his father let him wander, but over time he became concerned. The woods were dangerous. The father did not know what lurked there.

He decided to discuss the matter with his child. One day he took him aside and said, "You know, I have noticed that each day you walk into the woods. I wonder why do you go there?"

The boy said to his father, "I go there to find God."

"That is a very good thing," the father replied gently. "I am glad you are searching for God. But, my child, don't you know that God is the same everywhere?"

"Yes," the boy answered, "but I'm not."

DAVID J. WOLPE
Teaching Your Children about God

PART SEVEN

Freckles and Wrinkles

A grandmother and her little granddaughter, whose face was sprinkled with red freckles, spent the day at the zoo. The children were waiting in line to get their cheeks painted by a local artist who was decorating them with tiger paws. "You've got so many freckles, there's no place to paint!" a little boy in the line remarked. Embarrassed, the little girl dropped her head. Her grandmother knelt down next to her.

"I love your freckles," she said.

"Not me," the little girl cried.

"Well, when I was a little girl I always wanted freckles" she said, tracing her finger across her granddaughter's cheek. "Freckles are just beautiful."

The little girl looked up "Really?"

"Of course," said the Grandmother. "Why, just name me one thing that's prettier than freckles."

The little girl peered into her grandmother's smiling face. "Wrinkles," she answered softly.

AUTHOR UNKNOWN

Thumbelina Truth

Jeedus wuvs me,
For bydoe telws me,
Witto ones him ewong,
Day weak he stong.
Yes Jeedus wuvs me,
For bydoe telws me so.

Tears filled my eyes as I secretly overheard my just turned-two-year-old daughter singing this song to her doll. My wife and I had sung "Jesus Loves Me" to her a hundred times. She had recently started singing it with us. Now she was passing on to another what she had learned. Fumbowina (Thumbelina) received an imperfect verse of perfect truth shared from a loving heart.

Through my daughter, the Lord reminded me just how simple evangelism can be. Though our methods may be imperfect and our tongues stumble over just the right words, evangelism is sharing the truth of God's love in sincerity and compassion.

Can it be any simpler? Can anything be more important than teaching our children?

SCOTT K. STEPHANS
Noblesville, Ind.

Most Caring Child

Author and lecturer Leo Buscaglia once talked about a contest he was asked to judge. The purpose of the contest was to find the most caring child. The winner was a four-year-old child whose next door neighbor was an elderly gentleman who had recently lost his wife. Upon seeing the man cry, the little boy went into the old gentleman's yard, climbed onto his lap, and just sat there. When his mother asked him what he had said to the neighbor, the little boy said, "Nothing, I just helped him cry."

AUTHOR UNKNOWN

The Jesus Room

My husband, Ray, and I recently took our grandchildren to see their mother who was in Dearborn County Hospital recovering from surgery. We entered the hospital and headed down the hall. "There's Jesus' room," Jacob whispered. I glanced aside to see we were passing the hospital chapel. With three children in tow, we hurried on our way. Later I wondered about his statement. What had Jacob, five, put together in his thoughts that made the room remind him of Jesus? Somewhere, maybe from listening to his parents, Sunday school teachers, or his Christian day care and preschool, he reasoned what Jesus' room should look like.

When I returned to the hospital the next day I made a special point to visit the chapel. It is very much like a miniature church, Jacob's Jesus room. It is a pleasant, inviting room, somewhere you could communicate with God. I did.

The next time Jacob visited the hospital with his mother, he again spoke of the Jesus room. This time he asked his mother to stop. He hesitated by the door, somewhat in awe of the special room, then went in and chose to sit on the front pew. There he felt comfortable enough to pray with his mother.

Each Sunday we worship in our own Jesus room—our church. It contains, just as the hospital chapel does, candles, a Bible, a pulpit, pews, and the cross prominently displayed in front. Jacob associated these furnishings with Jesus. Do we, as adult members of the church, see and honor it as a place where

Jesus dwells? Do our words and actions while there show that we are in His sacred place? Too often we forget that church is a place to communicate with Jesus. We need to keep an atmosphere there that is inviting and reverent to us. Our church is Jesus' room.

DORIS BUTT
Sunman, Ind.

Who's that Knocking?

A nurse on the pediatric ward, before listening to the little ones' chests, would plug the stethoscope into their ears and let them listen to their own hearts. Their eyes would always light up with awe. But she never got a response to equal four-year-old David's. Gently she tucked the stethoscope in his ears and placed the disk over his heart. "Listen," she said. "What do you suppose that is?"

He drew his eyebrows together in a puzzled line and looked up as if lost in the mystery of the strange tap-tapping deep in his chest. Then his face broke out in a wondrous grin. "Is that Jesus knocking?" he asked.

AUTHOR UNKNOWN

Jesus in My Heart

A four-year-old was at the pediatrician's for a check-up. As the doctor looked in her ears and asked, "Do you think I'll find Big Bird in here?" The little girl stayed silent. Next, the doctor took a tongue depressor and looked down her throat. He asked, "Do you think I'll find the Cookie Monster down there?" Again, the little girl was silent. Then the doctor put a stethoscope to her chest. As he listened to her heartbeat, he asked, "Do you think I'll hear Barney in there?"

"Oh, no!" the little girl replied. "Jesus is in my heart. Barney's on my underpants."

AUTHOR UNKNOWN

The Youngest Evangelist

Eyes darting around the room, Kay entered the narthex. She was tightly clutching her registration card in her right hand. Kay had responded to a flier advertising Kids Club, which Columbia City United Methodist Church sent home through her elementary school. She quickly joined in the fun and fellowship.

At the end of the first day's program, Kay was left standing alone. No parent arrived to claim her. She had come on the school bus with friends and followed them to the church. Those children had walked home without her. Now tears began forming in her five-year-old eyes. I quickly walked over and put my arms around her shaking shoulders. Thus began a very special relationship in my life.

Taking her into my office, I scanned the registration forms and found an incomplete one with her name attached. With so many children that first day, no one had noticed the blank spaces on her form. No phone number was listed. When I questioned her, Kay responded, "We don't have one."

"No problem," I replied. "Just tell me where you live," as I noticed only the street name, not number, recorded.

"I don't remember," and she began to cry.

"No problem," I repeated. "Take my hand and we'll walk up and down the street until we find it."

As I began leading Kay outdoors, the phone rang. It soon became apparent I was needed in the office for awhile. Our choir director, Toni, had been listening to our conversation and offered to walk her home. Toni came back and shared that Kay lived in a very small apartment above a furniture store downtown.

The next week, Kay returned to Kids Club with her mother. She introduced Toni and me as her "two new friends." Her mother thanked us for taking such good care of Kay and offered to bake cookies for the club.

Kay was like a sponge absorbing water. She never got tired of hearing Bible stories. After Kids Club, she would come and ask me if those stories about Jesus were "really true." On other days of the week, she would stop in my office to give me a hug or to show me her school papers. Sometimes, when I walked downtown, I would see her playing in the street. She would be sitting on a curb playing with stones or a stick. I always stopped to chat with her.

Kay started inviting other children to come to Kids Club. Since she didn't have a phone at home, she would ask permission to use mine. Our secretary called her "our youngest evangelist."

One day I was working at my desk when she was using the telephone. She turned to me and said, "Pastor Heather, tell him you serve dinner." As I tried to explain to Kay that I couldn't do that, as we only served a snack—peanut butter sandwiches, fruit, or cheese and crackers, she interrupted me and pleaded, "But John will come if you say he'll get dinner. He's hungry just like me."

When I shared that information with our Kids Club staff, we began to change our focus. Feeding hungry kids became a priority. We also intentionally began an outreach to families who had less than many of our members.

Sometimes when we discovered a need, we referred the families to a helping agency. We also began a hands-on ministry to those families. That ministry has included providing back-to-school clothes for children, emergency food, getting a telephone installed, and granting scholarships to our new pre-school. When you minister to a child, you minister to a family!

HEATHER OLSON-BUNNELL
Decatur, Ind.

Kayla's Faith

Her name is Kayla and she was seven years old the fall she started second grade. In August she was riding her horse and fell off. The horse fell on her and the saddle horn pushed against her stomach.

Kayla is one of the bravest persons I have ever met. The consequences from her injury were serious. The trauma surgeon said surgery was necessary. The pancreas could have been split in two and the spleen damaged.

It was a Friday afternoon and my day off. I had just walked in the door of my home when I got the call. As soon as I got to the hospital, I prayed with Kayla and her family members gathered there. We talked about the times she went to Kids Club, Vacation Bible School, and Sunday School. I told her that when she went to surgery, her friend Jesus would be holding her hand, just like I was right now. Her mother, Aunt Susie, Grandma, and I were all holding hands in a circle as I prayed.

Kayla looked me straight in the eye and with supreme confidence said, "I know that, Pastor Heather."

Kayla meant it. She has a deep faith nurtured at St. Mark's UMC and in her family. Kayla's trust and belief that God will take care of her runs deep inside her.

The tears started to come into my eyes as she shared her faith with us. When I looked up at her mother, Aunt Susie, and Grandma, the tears were rolling down their faces too.

How calmly she went to surgery. When I looked into Kayla's eyes that evening, I saw such peace. Her face reminded me so much of the serene look of Mother Teresa's face I'd seen in pictures.

That kind of deep faith and trust doesn't just happen by itself. Her parents are great, both actively involved with their children and modeling the faith for them. Her grandparents are pretty special too, as well as extended family members. Kayla's total assurance that everything would be okay (and it was) came from a faith deep inside her. She knew she wasn't alone going through this ordeal. Her family and extended family in her church had instilled in her this basic trust that God would be there for her, and she believed it with all her heart.

Kayla very calmly went down to surgery with her parents on either side of her stretcher, and she kissed everyone good-bye. Surgery was less complicated than expected. Her colon was nearly torn in two, but was surgically repaired. All of us gathered in that waiting room left stronger in our own faith because of the faith a child had shown us.

HEATHER OLSON-BUNNELL
Decatur, Ind.

Afterword

Dear Friends of Children,

"Children are a gift from the Lord, they are a real blessing" (Ps. 127:3). The church of Jesus Christ needs children as much as the children need the church's ministry. God speaks through and to children. Through the years, God has brought many children into my life. My commitment to children and the poor comes from the "sermons" I have heard from the lips of these children. As you have read these stories, I pray that you were inspired and motivated, and are now eager to reach out with enthusiasm to children and the poor in each of your communities.

Reaching out to children was a radical act in Jesus' time. We are called today to reach out in this same way in Jesus' name.

Let the children come . . .

REV. HEATHER OLSON-BUNNELL
Chairperson, North Indiana Conference
United Methodist Bishops'
Task Force on Children and Poverty